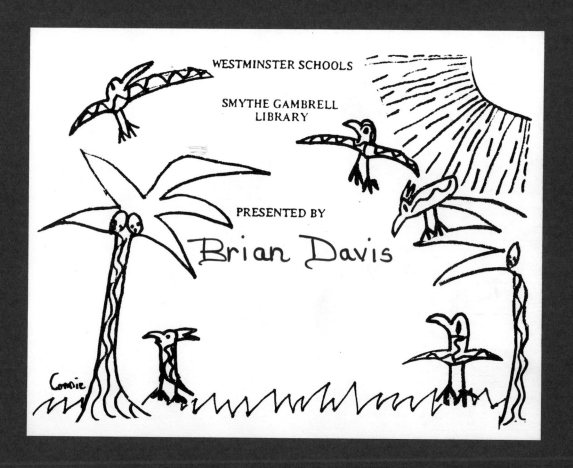

The
WINTER
OLYMPICS

Published by Creative Education, Inc.
123 South Broad Street, Mankato, MN 56001

Designed by Rita Marshall with the help of Thomas Lawton
Cover illustration by Rob Day, Lance Hidy Associates

Photography by Allsport, Nancy Battaglia, Bettman
Archive, Focus on Sports, Ken Graham, Globe Photos,
David Madison, Photri, Bob Thomas, Wide World Photos

Printed in the United States

Library of Congress Cataloging-in-Publication Data

Harris, Jack C.
   The Winter Olympics/by Jack C. Harris: edited by Michael E.
Goodman.
   p.   cm.—(Great moments in sports)
   Summary: Discusses the history of the Winter Olympics, the events,
and outstanding athletes over the years.
   ISBN 0-88682-317-X
   1. Winter Olympics—History—Juvenile literature.   2. Athletes—
Biography—Juvenile literature.   [1. Winter Olympics—
History.]   I. Goodman, Michael E.   II. Title.   III. Series.
GV841.5.H37   1989   89-27078
796.98—dc20   CIP
                                                            AC

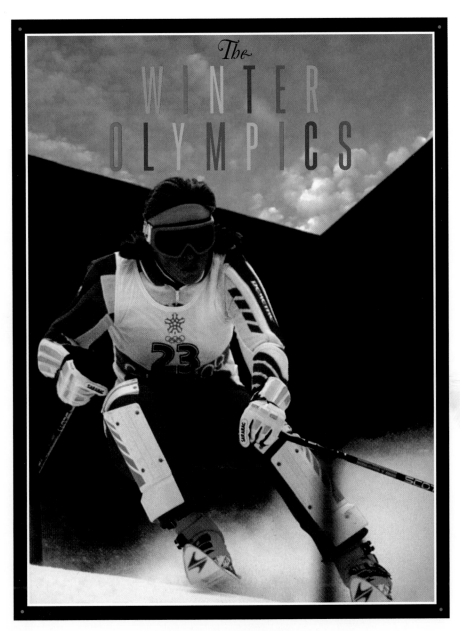

The WINTER OLYMPICS

JACK C. HARRIS

CREATIVE EDUCATION INC.

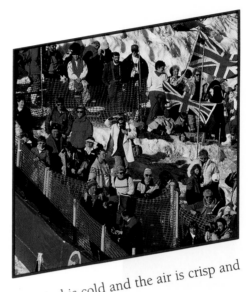

The wind is cold and the air is crisp and clear. Snow covers the ground and caps the mountains in the distance. Hundreds of colorful banners and flags wave in the chilly wind. Crowds of people move to and fro, ignoring the frigid temperatures. Through the earmuffs and scarves that cover everyone's ears, many different languages can be heard: English, French, Russian, German, Slovak, Swedish. . . .

Suddenly, a hush drops over the throng of people and all eyes turn upward. High on a mountain, a huge ramp has been constructed. It slopes at a steep incline down the mountainside. The ramp's end turns upward, aimed at nothing but midair. Ice covers the ramp from top to bottom. At its very top, a tiny figure stands. The crowd below catches a glimpse of his seven-foot-long skis hanging dangerously over the ramp's top edge. The crowd holds its breath as the ski jumper crouches low, tucking his chin onto his chest. He eyes the takeoff platform far below and takes a deep breath.

The man is Matty Nykanen from the small city of Jyväskylä in the icy coastal region of Finland. He is hundreds of miles from home today, jumping from a ramp atop a mountain near Sarajevo, Yugoslavia. What has brought him here? He has come for the chance to win a gold medal in the Winter Olympics, to be a winter hero.

The crowd below waited in anticipation as Matty sailed towards them.

Suddenly, Matty jumps forward and begins sailing along the ice-covered incline. Still in a crouched position, he ducks lower, reducing the wind's resistance as he speeds down the ramp. All eyes are on him as he flies off the platform at a tremendous speed and propels himself like a graceful bird into space.

Matty Nykanen is only one competitor in just one Winter Olympic event. In mountain areas nearby, daredevil skiers race straight down steep slopes at breakneck speed in the downhill event or zigzag gracefully in the slalom. Nordic skiers speed across challenging terrain and some even stop periodically to shoot rifles at distant targets. In the bobsled event, sledders race down runs carved out of ice, challenging the clock and risking their lives to determine who is the best combination of athlete and engineer. In packed ice arenas, figure skaters spin and leap, and hockey players push and pound.

The luge is another exciting Winter Olympic event.

From countries all over the world, competitors have come to see who is the fastest, the strongest, the most graceful, the most agile—the best. From their homelands, supporters have come to make up the enormous, cheering crowds. For many—especially those fans from wintry countries like Finland—these skiers, skaters, and sledders are national heroes. They are daring athletes who brave the weather and landscape time and again for their countries' sake and for their own personal thrill of victory.

9

Skiers race through the zig-zag slalom course.

HOW IT BEGAN

The first recorded great moment in Olympic history occurred in ancient Greece in 776 B.C. It was not a competition on skates or skis. It was a footrace of about 200 yards held on the plains of Olympia to honor Zeus, king of the Greek gods. Over the years, the games grew to include such events as chariot races, footraces, wrestling, discus throwing, jumping, and horseback riding. Athletes from all Greek city-states gathered to compete in the Olympics every four years. Wars were even stopped temporarily for the Olympics, which came to represent the highest ideals of sportsmanship. Gradually, however, the games lost their original purpose and became so corrupt that Emperor Theodosius I canceled them in A.D. 394.

The biathlon combines cross-country skiing with target shooting.

The Olympics were revived in 1896 under the leadership of Baron Pierre de Coubertin of France. At first the modern Olympics, like the ancient games, included no winter events. It wasn't until the 1908 Olympics in London that a winter sporting event was officially held, with both men and women competing in figure skating.

Although the next two Olympic Games were held in countries noted for their winter sports, Sweden and Belgium, it was not until 1924, when the first Winter Olympic Games were held in Chamonix, France, that winter sports became a regular part of the Olympics. At those first Winter Games, events included not only figure skating but hockey, speed skating, cross-country skiing, and ski jumping. As years have gone by, many Winter Olympic events have changed. Some have been removed from the Games altogether, and new ones have been added. A few of the events, such as the biathlon and the luge, may sound strange or unusual. But all of them are designed to test the Olympians' athletic skills, training, and discipline. And each of them, at one time or another, have given Winter Olympic fans a great moment to remember.

SHINING STARS ON ICE

Very few people who attended the first Winter Olympics in Chamonix paid much attention to an eleven-year-old figure skater from Norway named Sonja Henie. She came in eighth, and last, place that year, but she gained valuable experience. Four years later, now a graceful teenager, Sonja was back in Saint Moritz, Switzerland. This time, she would give a performance that the figure-skating judges and the audience would not forget.

Traditionally, men skaters were supposed to do all the leaps and spins, while women were expected to feature gliding and grace in their free-skating performances. The women skaters sailed around the ice to music, but their programs were not physically challenging and their movements seldom seemed to match the notes that were being played. Sonja Henie changed all of that.

At Saint Moritz, Henie combined skating with ballet dancing as she performed to the music of Tchaikovsky's *Swan Lake*. She leapt and spun and dipped across the ice in perfect time to the romantic music. The audience at the rink cheered. But would the judges be as impressed? The answer was soon known. Six of the seven judges cast first-place votes for Sonja, and she was awarded the gold medal.

Henie captured two more gold medals in 1932 at Lake Placid, New York, and in 1936 at Garmisch–Partenkirchen, Germany. In those eight years, Sonja not only made Olympic history with her three gold medals but also changed the sport of figure skating forever.

Sonja Henie gave a dazzling performance at Saint Moritz.

By the time she retired from competitive skating, Sonja Henie was known and loved all around the world. She had accumulated 1,470 cups, medals, and trophies in addition to her Olympic medals. She had also inspired a new generation of women skaters to be more daring and exciting on the ice.

After 1936, the next time the Winter Olympics were held was in 1948 because the 1940 and 1944 Games were canceled due to World War II. The greatest moment in the 1948 Olympics, which was held again at Saint Moritz, was once again provided by a figure skater. This time, however, it was a young American skater named Dick Button. The eighteen-year-old Button was leading the competition going into his freestyle program. He had learned a new, exciting double-spin jump and wanted to try it out. But he was nervous. What if he fell attempting the jump and the judges lowered his score? Button decided that if he held back he would not be a true champion. He tried the jump, and it went perfectly. It was a gold-medal performance.

History repeated itself in 1952. This time, Button had learned a triple jump but debated whether to play it safe in the freestyle event to preserve his lead or go for broke and use his new move. Button decided to take the risk. Skating swiftly backward, he left his feet for his triple loop and then panicked. He couldn't remember which shoulder to lead with on the jump. Almost by instinct, he chose correctly and executed a perfect three-spin move, landing on the same skate from which he had taken off. The fans in the arena in Oslo, Norway, all rose to give Button a standing ovation. Once again, he had proved himself a true gold medalist.

Dick Button became one of the greatest figure skating champions of all time.

Years later another American, Scott Hamilton, won the Olympic gold medal.

Norse fans were proud when Sonja Henie won her gold medals, and they cheered wildly for Dick Button in the ice-skating rink in Oslo. But a few days after Button's performance, they really went crazy. The date was February 18, 1952, and it has gone down as one of the greatest moments in the history of Norwegian sports.

Hjalmar Anderson

14

Norway is a very cold country, and most Norse children grow up knowing how to skate and ski. So it's not unusual that some of the greatest skiers, ski jumpers, and speed and figure skaters in Olympic history have come from Norway. In fact, ski jumping was first perfected by a Norwegian named Jacob Thulin Thams, who won the first gold medal in ski jumping in the 1924 Olympics. And in each Olympics between 1924 and 1948, Norwegian jumpers also captured the gold.

Vegard Ulvang

On February 18, 1952, Norse fans gathered at the ski-jumping facility, at the speed-skating rink, and along the cross-country skiing course. Their national stars were competing in events in all three locations. The cheering began early, as Hjalmar Andersen won the 1,500-meter speed-skating event for the first of his three gold medals during the Olympics. A few hours later, Hallgeir Brenden, a lumberjack and farmer from the tiny town of Tyrsil, came in first in the eighteen-kilometer cross-country skiing race.

Hallgeir Brenden

One final event was still to be settled for the day. It was the Nordic combined competition, in which participants must both ski jump and race along an eighteen-kilometer cross-country skiing course. Norway's Simon Slattvik, who

Simon Slattvik won Norway's third gold medal in a single day.

was leading at the end of the ski-jumping competition, put on a strong finishing sprint in the ski race to win the gold medal.

Three Olympic gold medals in one day for Norway's athletes! People all over Oslo were thrilled. Norse fans at the Olympic site hugged each other and danced around. Most Norse men and women who were working had been listening to Olympic bulletins on radios. Now they left their jobs and gathered in the streets of the city to celebrate this great moment. For the next few hours, no work was accomplished in Oslo. It was like a national holiday. It was a time to celebrate athletic achievements and national pride.

SPORTSMANSHIP

Olympic fans in Norway and around the world cheer not only for their national heroes but for all of the great athletes that take part in the many events. They appreciate the athletes' skill, competitive spirit, and good sportsmanship.

Italian bobsledder Eugenio Monti was a true Olympic hero known for both his talent and his fine character. Monti was a fierce competitor who devoted twelve years of his life to winning a gold medal in the two-man bobsled event. In the

1956 Winter Olympics in Cortina, Italy, Monti and his partner came in a close second behind another Italian team. Eight years later, at the 1964 Winter Olympics in Innsbruck, Austria, Monti and a new partner were once again in the running for the gold medal. Monti's chances looked better when the British team in first place experienced problems with its sled. A bolt holding one of the sled's runners in place had broken off. The British team thought it might have to drop out of the competition.

Eugenio Monti devoted years of his life to the two-man bobsled competition.

Monti, who was waiting for his final run on the course, heard about the problem. He removed a bolt from his own team's sled and brought it to the shed where the British kept their equipment. He even helped his opponents repair their sled. With the new runner bolt in place, the Englishmen retained their lead and won the gold medal, while Monti and his partner finished in third place less than a second behind the winners.

17

The four-man bobsled is another great test of skill.

In the 1968 Olympics, Monti, then forty years old, decided to make one more try for the coveted gold medal. His team was trailing by one-tenth of a second after the first three runs down the course. They had one more chance. Monti drove his sled to a course record time of 1:10.05 (one minute, ten seconds, and five one-hundredth seconds). He thought he had the gold for sure. Then the first-place West German team made its final run. The Germans' run was exactly one-tenth of a second slower than Monti's had been. The two teams were tied. The judges decided, however, to award the gold to the team with the fastest run of the day, and that was Monti's.

A few days later, Monti won another gold medal when he piloted the Italian four-man bobsled to victory by less than one-tenth of a second over an Austrian team. With his two medals hanging around his neck, Monti told the cheering fans, "Now I can retire a happy man."

Lydia Skoblikova, 1964.

THE GOOD-LUCK PIN

Olympic champions like Eugenio Monti are noted for their athletic ability and their sportsmanship. Some of them are also a little superstitious. One of the great moments in Olympic speed-skating history involves a bit of superstition. In 1964, the U.S. speed-skating coach was a man named Leo Freisinger, who had placed third in the 1936 Olympics. Freisinger's wife was a good friend of Russian skating champion Lydia Skoblikova and had given her friend a good-luck pin. Wearing the pin, Skoblikova won a record four gold medals in the 1964 Innsbruck Olympics.

U.S. Hockey team "Miracle on ice" in 1980

Four years later, U.S. skater Dianne Holum also wore one of Mrs. Freisinger's pins. She won only two bronze medals that year but came back to win a gold and silver in two different events in 1972.

The history of these good-luck pins has one final chapter. Dianne Holum passed along some of her good luck to her best pupil. In 1980, that student, Eric Heiden, put on perhaps the greatest Olympic speed-skating performance of all time when he won gold medals in all five men's speed-skating events at the Lake Placid Games. No other Olympic athlete, in the Summer or Winter Games, has ever won five gold medals in individual events during the course of one Olympic Games.

THE FLAMBOYANT FRENCHMAN

Eric Heiden swept all of the speed-skating medals in 1980, but he was not the first Olympic athlete to make a clean sweep in his sport at the Winter Olympics. In 1956, an Austrian skier named Toni Sailer won all three gold medals in Alpine, or downhill, skiing. Then, in 1968, Frenchman Jean-Claude Killy duplicated Sailer's feat.

The top American men's skater at Innsbruck was Terry McDermott, a barber from Essexville, Michigan. McDermott asked his coach's wife if she had another good-luck pin for him. She gave him a pin, which he wore as he upset the best Norwegian and Russian skaters to win the gold medal in the 500-meter event.

Eric Heiden gave one of the greatest speed-skating performances ever.

Killy was born and raised in Val d'Isère, France, a town noted for skiing. He began skiing at the age of seven and was already competing in major international events by the time he was sixteen. Killy was well known throughout the world not only for his great skiing ability but also for his fun-loving nature. He loved to clown around. One time, for a joke, while taking part in a ski-jumping competition, he caused a sensation by dropping his pants in midair and landing with his long underwear visible to the crowd.

Twenty years after Killy, Pirmin Zurbriggen won the downhill event.

In 1968, when the Winter Olympics were held in France, however, Killy was all business. The French fans were counting on him to win all three Alpine skiing gold medals. Killy didn't disappoint them in the downhill race or the giant slalom. Then came the slalom race, in which skiers must not only speed as quickly as possible down the mountain but also zigzag through some fifty-five to seventy-five gates.

At first, Austrian skier Karl Schranz was declared the winner of the slalom race held on an extremely foggy course, with Killy placing second. But after a short delay, the judges determined that Schranz had failed to pass through several gates near the top of the foggy course. Schranz was disqualified, and Killy had his third gold medal and a sweep of the Alpine events.

Hubert Strolz captured the gold medal in 1988.

The 1980 Olympics in Lake Placid, New York, didn't feature an athlete with the charisma of Killy, but it did have some great moments of its own. Typically, Olympians from the United States have often done well in the Summer Olympics, but the Winter Games usually have been dominated by European stars. In 1980, however, things were different. Speed skater Eric Heiden, as previously mentioned, put on the greatest individual performance ever by an Olympian when he won his five gold medals. American fans cheered loudly for Heiden, but they gave their loudest applause to an unlikely group of heroes, the U.S. ice hockey team.

The hockey team from the Soviet Union was heavily favored to win the gold at Lake Placid, while the Americans were not expected to take any medal. Much of the Russian squad had been playing together for eight years, and this was their third Olympics as a team. They had previously won the gold medal in both 1972 and 1976. The American team, on the other hand, consisted mostly of college players.

26

Three days before the Olympics began, the Russians had played the Americans in an exhibition match and had won 10–3. So when the two teams faced off in the semifinal round of the hockey competition, few people expected the U.S. team would have a chance.

Most people thought the U.S. team would be easily defeated by the Russians.

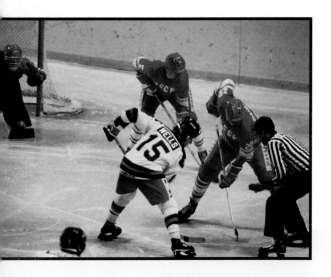

The Russians had the only score in the second period, but that lead disappeared when Johnson scored his second goal midway through the final stanza. Less than two minutes later, American captain Mike Eruzione, using a Russian player as a screen, sent a thirty-foot slap shot into the goal. Suddenly, the U.S. team was ahead. With their fans cheering wildly from the stands, the Americans held off all Russian attempts to tie the game. The next day, newspapers throughout the U.S. carried front-page stories about the "miracle on ice."

The Russians scored first on a deflected shot, but the U.S. squad tied the score five minutes later. The Soviets tallied again moments later and held a 2–1 lead with just seconds left in the first period. Then an American player took a wild last-second shot that rebounded off the pads of the outstanding Soviet goalie, Vladimir Myshkin. American winger Mark Johnson pushed the rebound under Myshkin's pads with one second to go. The score was only tied as the two teams left the ice, but the American players were cheering and hugging, while the Russians were clearly shocked.

The Russians were stunned to find themselves losing to the U.S.

Even with this exciting and thrilling win, the American team knew that if they lost their last game to Finland they could still come in third because of the Olympic scoring system. The Americans overcame a 2–1 Finnish lead with three goals in the final period to win the game and the gold. The nation went wild. For one day, at least, hockey replaced baseball as America's national pastime!

SARAJEVO AND CALGARY

While the American hockey players were the heroes on ice in the 1980 Olympics, two exciting figure skaters earned much of the applause at Sarajevo, Yugoslavia, in 1984.

In 1988, Alberto Tomba won the gold medal in the giant slalom race.

Scott Hamilton's victory at Sarajevo was not a big surprise. After all, the American figure skater had won three straight world championships in the three years before the Olympics. But no one who knew Scott when he was a little boy would have believed he could be an athletic star. When he was two years old, Scott stopped growing normally, and doctors didn't know why. His desperate

parents finally thought that getting Scott involved with athletics might help him grow. So, at age nine, Scott began skating. Amazingly, the tiny, thin child began to grow a little at a time and became stronger. He also began to win skating competitions. In 1980, he was fifth in the Lake Placid Olympics. Then

Scott Hamilton won two Olympic gold medals in figure skating.

in 1984, he struck gold. The five-foot two-inch, 108-pound champion was now the giant of the skating world!

While Scott Hamilton was leading the way among male figure skaters in 1984, and again in 1988 in Calgary, a German teenager named Katarina Witt amazed audiences viewing the women's competition with her daring costumes and her even more daring spins and jumps on the ice. Sonja Henie would have been proud of Witt's grace and strength. Performing to classical music, Witt executed several perfect jumps and other exciting moves to win the admiration of both the crowds and the judges.

WINTER OLYMPIC CHAMPIONS

Who are the champions of the Winter Olympics? They are the men and women who have combined strength and grace and determination in their effort to defeat both their competition and the difficult elements of nature in the winter. They glide or speed over ice, sail along or above snow, and challenge gravity in a series of daredevil maneuvers. They are top athletes who go all out to win but who also—like the Italian bobsledder Eugenio Monti—assist and cooperate with their opponents in the spirit of Olympic sportsmanship. That's what the Olympics is all about: competition and cooperation between athletes and between nations.

Katarina Witt's performances captivated audiences and judges alike in 1988.

Everyone who competes in a Winter Olympic event has proven himself or herself to be a champion and a part of history. As Clifford H. Buck, a former president of the U.S. Olympic Committee, said, "We are proud of the athletes who demonstrated excellence in the most rigorous of worldwide competition. They are deserving of the highest tribute because they demonstrated the will to win, the self-discipline, and the willingness to sacrifice which characterize a champion."

Matty Nykanen had been a champion. He had been a gold medalist at Sarajevo in 1984. But now, as he sailed into the air, 1984 was the furthest thing from his mind. His entire concentration was focused on this one jump.

High in the air, Matty leans far forward over the skis so that his body and skis are both parallel to the ground. Farther he flies, but his speed and height are lessening quickly. Gravity is pulling him down. He stretches and leans more, trying to keep his body aloft as long as he can.

As he touches down, his knees are bent and his arms are outstretched at his sides for balance. It's a perfect landing, and the crowd explodes with thunderous cheers. Judges rush forward to determine how far Matty has flown. Then a scoreboard announces the good news: It's a new Winter Olympics record! Finnish fans in the crowd and at home cheer their new national hero. He is an Olympic champion and, for this great moment, the best ski jumper in the world.

Finland's Matty Nykanen worked very hard to win.